Little Book of Questions & Answers

Nature

Copyright © 1992 Publications International, Ltd. All rights reserved. This book may not be reproduced or quoted in whole or in part by mimeograph or any other printed or electronic means, or for presentation on radio, television, videotape, or film without written permission from:

Louis Weber, C.E.O.
Publications International, Ltd.
7373 North Cicero Avenue
Lincolnwood, Illinois 60646

Permission is never granted for commercial purposes.

Manufactured in U.S.A.

8 7 6 5 4 3 2 1

ISBN: 1-56173-469-1

Contributing Writer: Teri Crawford Jones

Illustrations: T. F. Marsh

PUBLICATIONS INTERNATIONAL, LTD.

Where does the moon go in the daytime?
Sometimes the moon is on the other side of the earth where we can't see it. Sometimes it is in the daytime sky, but the sunlight makes it difficult to find in the bright sky.

Will the sun ever burn out?
The sun will not burn out for another five billion years. That's a longer time than we can imagine! Our sun is strong and healthy. It will rise every morning and set every evening as it always has.

Why does the sun hurt our eyes?
Bright lights hurt our eyes—and the sun is the brightest light of all! It is so bright that it is very, *very* dangerous to look at it. Scientists use special telescopes to study the sun.

Why does the moon change shape?
The moon reflects light from the sun. Sometimes the sun faces the moon and we see the whole, full moon. Sometimes the sun shines on one side of the moon and we see a half-moon.

How did the stars get in the sky?
Stars are like huge balls of fire. A star begins as swirling dust and *gases* (air is made of gases) that get hotter and hotter as they swirl in space. When they flame and burn, a star is born!

Where do colors go at night?
We need light to see colors. When it's dark, our eyes can't see colors. If the moon is bright, we may see some colors, but they are different from daytime colors.

Where does the sun go when it sets?
The earth turns in space as it moves around the sun. As we turn, the sun seems to move across the daytime sky. At sunset, the sun is beginning to shine on the other side of the world.

What are clouds made of?
Clouds are made of tiny droplets of water. The droplets are light enough to float in the air. Clouds feel like cold, wet air. Fog is a kind of cloud that is close to the ground.

Why do we see our breath on a cold day?
Our breath is moist. That means there are very, very small droplets of water in the air we breathe out. When our moist breath hits the cold air, the droplets freeze and turn into a little cloud.

How are icicles made?
When a winter day warms up a little, the snow and ice start to melt and drip. When it gets cold enough to freeze again, the drips turn to ice. When this happens over and over, icicles are made.

What kind of snow makes good snowballs?
Very cold air is dry. On really cold days, snowflakes do not stick together well. On warmer days, the snowflakes are moist and *do* stick together well. This snow is best for snowballs!

Why doesn't sunlight feel warm in the winter?
The earth is tilted as it spins in space. In winter, we are tilted away from the sun. Even though we get sunlight, it is not as strong as the summer sunlight when we are tilted toward the sun.

Why is thunder sometimes loud and sometimes soft?
Thunder is made by lightning. When lightning is close by, the thunder is loud. When lightning is far away, the thunder is not as loud.

Where does rain come from?
Clouds are made of tiny water droplets. When the air in the sky cools, the droplets cling together and get bigger. At last, they are too heavy to stay in the sky and they fall. It is raining!

What makes the colors in a rainbow?
Sunlight is made of red, orange, yellow, green, blue, dark blue, and violet. Raindrops break the light into these colors if the sun shines through them the right way.

Where do hurricanes come from?
A hurricane is born far out over the ocean. Its stormy winds grow stronger as it moves across the water. Some hurricanes die before they reach land, but others do reach land. They are dangerous!

Why are tornadoes funnel-shaped?
A tornado is made of spinning, twisting wind. The twisting gives the wind a funnel shape. Dust and dirt give it a dark color.

How can a tornado wreck one house, but not the next?
The part of a tornado that touches the ground, the stem, can be very narrow. A house in the path of the stem will be damaged. If the stem doesn't touch the next house, that house may be safe.

What is a volcano?
A volcano is like a mountain with a hole that reaches deep down into the earth. Down there, it is hot enough to melt rock! When a volcano erupts, the melted rock boils out.

What is lava?
The melted rock that comes out of a volcano is called lava. The lava runs down the sides of the volcano and inches across the land. Lava burns everything in its way.

Are volcanoes dangerous to people?
Volcanoes can be dangerous, but scientists who study volcanoes know when a volcano is going to erupt. People usually have time to pack up and get away before there is any danger.

Are mosquitoes good for anything?
Believe it or not, mosquitoes *are* good for something! They are food for larger animals like bats, birds, and other insects. Without mosquitoes, these animals would have a hard time surviving.

Why do ants live in big groups?
Ants live and work together to survive. Some hunt for food, some build the anthill, some have the babies, and some care for the young. Ants cooperate with each other!

Why do bees sting?
Bees use their stingers to protect themselves. Most people—and animals—know that many bees sting, so we stay away. Bees are not mean. They are just trying to survive in nature.

Why are flowers different colors?
Insects and birds help flowers spread their pollen to make new flowers. The different colors help insects and birds find the flowers they like.

How do plants spread their seeds?
Some plants have pods that open with a *pop!* that throws the seeds. Some seeds stick to animal fur or people's clothes and are carried away. Some seeds are light and are carried away by the wind.

If cows eat grass, why don't we?
Cows have a different kind of stomach than people. A cow's stomach can digest (make food from) grass. A human stomach would have a hard time digesting grass. Besides, grass does not taste good to people.

What do trees live on?
Trees are plants. Just like other plants, their leaves make food from sunlight. Their roots soak up water and other things from the soil.

Why do some trees change color in autumn?
Many trees "sleep" in winter when there isn't enough sunlight to make food. Their leaves fall off late in autumn. Before they fall, they may turn yellow, orange, or red.

Does it hurt a tree if its branch is broken?
A tree doesn't feel pain. But if a big branch is broken or cut off, the tree could die. There are "tree doctors," though. These people can help save a tree's life.

Can a lake dry up?
When the weather is hot and it has not rained for a long, long time, a lake may dry up. The fish in the lake die and the animals that live near the lake must look for other water.

Where do rivers begin?
Many rivers begin as small mountain streams made of newly melted snow and fresh rain water. As the stream travels, it is joined by other streams. It grows and grows until it becomes a big river.

How do fish get into a lake?
Some fish swim into a lake from a river. Other fish were born in the lake. Still others might have been raised on a special fish farm. Farm-raised fish are put in the lake by people.

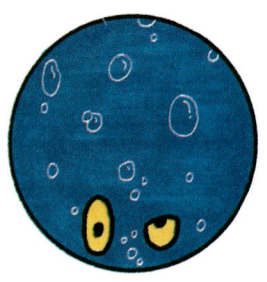

How deep is the ocean?
In some places, called trenches, the ocean may be seven miles deep. The highest mountain on land is not that high! The water down there is very cold and very dark.

What is a seashell?
Shells that wash onto the beach were once home to small sea animals like clams or oysters. These animals' shells help protect their soft bodies from pounding surf and hungry sea otters.

Why is the ocean blue?
Far from shore, the ocean's water is clear. It looks blue because the blue sky is reflected in the water. On a dark day, the ocean may look gray or dark green.

Why do waves tug at our ankles?
Even though an ocean wave may be small, it can still have a strong pull called an undertow. When the water flows back to the sea, it takes sand and shells with it.

Why are some waves bigger than others?
Storms at sea make big waves. Sometimes the waves calm down before they reach land, but sometimes they do not. Some storm waves can damage the houses built near the beach.

What is seaweed?
Seaweed is a plant. Most seaweed clings to rocks, letting its *fronds,* which are like leaves, float on or near the surface of the ocean. Seaweed provides food and shelter for many sea creatures.

Where does sand come from?

Grains of sand are made over a long, long time. Sand comes from rocks, minerals, coral, and shells. These things are tumbled around by ocean waves and blown by the wind. They are broken into tiny pieces. The wind and water never stop pounding and blowing the grains of sand.